SOFT KEYS

SOFT KEYS

Michael Symmons Roberts

CAPE POETRY

Published by Jonathan Cape 2009

4 6 8 10 9 7 5 3

Copyright © Michael Symmons Roberts 1993

Michael Symmons Roberts has asserted his right under the Copyright, Designs
and Patents Act 1988 to be identified as the author of this work

First published in Great Britain in 1993 by
Martin Secker & Warburg
This edition published in 2009 by
Jonathan Cape
Random House, 20 Vauxhall Bridge Road,
London SW1V 2SA

www.rbooks.co.uk

Addresses for companies within The Random House Group Limited can be found
at: www.randomhouse.co.uk.offices.htm

The Random House Group Limited Reg. No. 954009

A CIP catalogue record for this book is available from the British Library

ISBN: 9780224090018

The Random House Group Limited supports The Forest Stewardship
Council (FSC), the leading international forest certification organisation. All our
titles that are printed on Greenpeace approved FSC certified paper carry the FSC logo.
Our paper procurement policy can be found at http://www.rbooks.co.uk/environment

Mixed Sources
Product group from well-managed
forests and other controlled sources
www.fsc.org Cert no. TT-COC-2139
© 1996 Forest Stewardship Council

Typeset in Bembo by Palimpsest Book Production Limited,
Grangemouth, Stirlingshire
Printed and bound in Great Britain by
MPG Books Ltd, Bodmin, Cornwall

CONTENTS

ACKNOWLEDGEMENTS

Acknowledgements are due to the following:

Ambit, Gregory Anthology (Hutchinson), London Magazine, Poetry Wales, Times Literary Supplement, Verse

'Hang-Gliders' was broadcast on 'Kaleidoscope', Radio 4.

From the night-shift cement works,
dust built on fields, seeped
into buildings, coughed me awake.

It fused with fallen rain
to make a crust so thin one heel
could break the landscape open.

I held my breath, the sheet
pulled up across my face,
afraid my lungs would set.

When you woke me, the dust
cleared. I heard dawn crack,
smelt on your hands burst

fruit. Old skins, bruised black,
you split with thumbnails, found
seeds of new bodies inside intact.

I was born believing, able to see sounds as
    colours.
The underfeeding in this camp has magnified
    that faculty
so birds spout northern lights, and guards
    shout ribbons.

In the misery of this bitter bright Silesian
    December
I long for an end to time, a finish to the mystery
    of God,
the coarse-grained setting of faith into a
    blinding fact.

A sympathetic guard brings pencils and
    manuscript.
We can only make with what we have; in God
    I have it all,
but here a three-stringed cello, piano, violin
    and clarinet.

Its world premiere will take place in a
    washroom,
where I know this French and Polish audience
    of peasants,
doctors and priests will be the most attentive
    I have seen.

We have all felt the same last vital forces
    stirring,
moving through the camp like water did before
    the pipes froze,

the promise of all I have hoped for, have loved
 and still love.

Though it is not for us to know or guess,
 perhaps as we begin
to play the eighth and final movement –
 beyond the day of rest
after creation into ceaseless light and peace –

the end may come, the seventh angel crowned
 with a rainbow,
one foot in flames on the Pacific Ocean,
 the other
burning without melting, light as a leaf on
 Silesian snow.

THE BOTANICAL GARDENS

The Botanical Gardens are closed
for the winter. The beds are all black.
The shrubs are sprung like wire traps.
Through the scrollwork gates we see
the vanilla-painted ice-cream house
being licked dirty by the rain.

The tide has deserted the marine lake.
The peacocks have been stuffed
and boxed, their tails now hats and fans.
The empty iron coops rattle
out of shape. The last of the season's
bread swells and melts uneaten.

Only the glasshouse keeps its insides
green. Water runs like a brass rail
through it, air too rich to breathe.
Our gloves have frozen to the gates.
All we can see of the glasshouse
is a jet of smoke from across the lake.

REPLICA

Starting with this bowl of fruit,
he decided to build a replica world
out of matchsticks. It would
be fully working and life-size.

The apple was his first failure.
Its cool varnish, imperfect shape
and inaccurate colour all
added up to fake fruit.

As the nights drew in he did too.
He monitored all his bodily functions,
checked and double-checked,
kept on working.

He struck and blew them out,
cut off the heads that piled up
like peppercorns, set another wood
wick to an imitation orange.

Planning ahead, he mulled over
Europe, its technical problems –
rivers, animals. The room's smell
sharpened with phosphorus.

Barefoot, and the gum trees letting go
a secondary, slower fall of rain.
Unable to believe in the soul,
he brings body and mind to his garden
in the hope that a faculty equal
to this moment may seed and grow.

A soul's the only place deep enough
to give thanks for a found daughter
you have never seen, whisked off
to lead a real life in another house;
and a parallel spectral one here
where she grew up stern, mysterious.

The two great moments in his past
he gave away too soon, the first to brothers
carpeting a new Kingdom Hall
before the outside walls
were up – who smiled, called the others
to spread it even further; and the last

he took straight to a telephone,
and dialled through his address book.
Now, but now, he rubs leaves with fingers,
sniffs out the orange from the lemon,
holds still as two grey and pink galahs
tap the feed tray with alternate beaks.

To hold this news against the palate
is to make the lawn he cut
from bush a garden party for the prolix
waiting dead, up from their hammocks
light and thin as fibre-optics,
to compare his limbo with their hiatus.

BEHEMOTH

Until then, small acts of rebellion
had sufficed to keep him going.

Queuing all night he would buy
the last of the few fish to survive

the journey this far inland,
and take it, wet-scaling his hand,

back to the apartment, neighbours
drooling as it swam the stairs.

He would study its eyes for hints
about the sea, water prints.

He would put it on a plate
and in siren-coloured oils, paint

himself poised, about to eat it.
Then he'd feed it to the cat.

For days he'd watch the new fish
harden to eternal life, then stash

the canvas under his mattress,
its hope seeping upwards

into his shallow sleep, soundless
crystallising in his eye corners.

It was like defying gravity,
defying death to leave the closed city.

First light, guns clearing catarrh.
He packed nothing, stole a car,

drove out through the districts
on a planned route, back-streets,

avoiding the Boulevard of Victory
which split the people precisely

like naked fruit-halves into two.
Foot flat down, but a slow

escape, the car tampered with,
doctored, put on half-life.

He drove an hour beyond
the last street, the last sound

that was not his own,
then he turned and looked behind.

Only now, at this distance,
could he see, in full magnificence,

the statue, the Man for Eternity,
pointing out towards history.

He kept driving until
the sputter of the last drop of fuel

halted him so far outside
the city that the blue-veined head

of the marble colossus had set
below the horizon. He feared

it might rise again tomorrow
so he walked until he knew

it had gone. As a child
he was forced to march for miles

in uniform around its base,
the great shoes, but its face

he'd never seen before,
an endless colourless stare

which put the stars in their
places. Behemoth cast a shadow

which scanned the metropolis
when the sun shone, entered houses

through windows, or bodies
through the cracks between eyelids.

SOFT KEYS

In Florida they're islands, if you're 21
today they're cast in cake, but if a keystone
was, all domes would cave to rubble,
so the keys to our abyss are hard to find.
It's key to be soft on piano, to pedal,
gloving the hammers for delicate tones,
but the bunch which opens on to calm

seas or true wisdom swings like giblets
heavy frozen, snaps in the lock and fills it;
the single one that lets you in
to someone's heart is often softer than you
thought, whilst those that used to wind
clocks tight and once kept day and night
in place are muzzy with dust and neglect.

As we praise the timing of quartz,
the keys to praise are held by birds
who scutter over their majors and minors
for he who unlocks hell and heaven.
The key to those binary soft ons and offs
of a computer is a single finger's
weight which teeters on the edge of thought,

the edge of a letter being born – it was.
And though a wedge for splitting wood or stone
must be spot on or else it bends
or shatters like the doors of death,
the dry winged fruits that ash trees send
to ground are such perfection of design
they open up the earth and rise.

So scratch some grooves into a wall
to make the final coat of plaster stick,
then pick up all these keys and try
the softest, that like skeletons can open
anything, but with much greater secrecy,
so all our locks are really ready-picked
and we just have to use the handles.

SCRAP METAL

The whinings of light planes
half wake me. In my sleep-half
the sky fills with so many
that their wings clack together
like beaks, bringing them down
in the field behind the house.

The rooks in the end trees
racket amongst themselves.
The house shifts on its rust
mattress of scrap metal.
The soil beneath is gorged
with bolts, chains and spokes.

I tear off finger-long strips
of the blue and gold patterned
wallpaper by the bed. Underneath,
the old paint feels cold.
I decide to paint my room
completely orange – windows too.

The hill in the rooks' field
is a long-barrow for motor-bikes.
Sometimes in the night,
I hear one spark up
like a distant throat,
then settle again.

SWAN-UPPING

Hearing this music is like eating
too many sweets; visitors don't stay
for long, just take in a few rides,
a pot-shot at a prize, see a freak.

It's too hot to hang around anyway,
the heat came too quickly, beating
unusually hard, tanning hides
or plain burning, leaving insides weak.

So most visits are flying, and some
are disappointed to discover
they are not children, cannot be,
the fair is far too small.

It's all in full swing this afternoon
when heads turn to the river
like weather-vanes to see
what's causing the kerfuffle.

It's swans, some in baskets,
some in boats roped down ready
to be hauled on the dry, sanded
planks of Turk's boatyard. They yell

so that everyone will notice,
and they do. As each is landed,
its wings and soul are clipped until
every swan is done, and set free.

One man is shy, or just discreet,
holding a huge swan and its basket
in front of his head to hide
his true identity.

A voice from the temporary
bridge 'Hey, move the bird aside
so I can get you in this snapshot.'
The bridge is buckling in the heat.

It was designed to last ten years,
but has been there twice
that time. The lensman starts to take
the scene, shouts down again,

but the subject cranes his white
neck round, opens his beak
and says 'No' in no uncertain
terms, 'No pictures please.'

When the job's done, the officials
ground their boats, pull them out
like fish hooked by their noses,
already gutted. They tip the dregs.

Open windows of riverfront houses
are stuffed as people pivot on sills
to get a better view of it.
Some find ladders, wooden legs,

climb up on to roofs or halfway
up creepered walls, clinging
with suckers they never guessed
they had, but are glad of now.

Some of the swans, ungainly guests,
whiter than finest laundry,
slowly sway towards the fairground.
Bearded children, snake women

and centaurs crawl out of their
highly-painted woodwork.
A smaller, lighter bird unseen
above mistakes the greatest fair

in town for a sticky, leftover
heap of coloured sweet papers,
static in the windless bake,
but the worlds wisest man

has warned colleagues and visitors
alike to stand completely still.
'One swan, if it takes a dislike,
can break your arm like a lolly stick.'

They stop the rides, cut the music
and watch as the swans amble inshore
to be fed by the popcorn seller
who is only too pleased to oblige.

For anyone who casts an eye
in other than the main direction,
say, downstream, a luminous patina
on the dark water

is inching its quiet way
round a far meander, taking in
boats, overhanging branches, even
a swan not caught yet.

When the fuss dies down the rides
creak into action in rough
time with flat music. One crank faster
would ease so much tension.

As the clipped swans slide
into cool water a Florentine figure,
perhaps a woman carrying cushions,
steps into a boat and casts off.

COMPLINE

Sustainer, who brings days by choice,
who cries with everyone who cries;
who gave it flavour, yet took milk
like any gasping baby does,
who knows the empty want of milk –
by hearing all, give all a voice.

Comforter, spirit of solace,
protect the joyful from their dreams
which seed in darkness fears of loss;
show us the beauty that redeems,
make purpose from our aimlessness –
by seeing all, give all a face.

HOSEA THOMAS IN THE
REALM OF MIRACLES

'Do you want to be healed?' (John 5:6)

I

Hosea Thomas cried up silently to God.
His soul had never yet slunk out
as late dogs barked, through the back door
to the scrap fields by the railway line,
to be cherished by her patient lover
while the left house slumbered behind.

No. But Hosea clung, still believed –
He asked for saffron and cinnamon,
asked that his soul, sweet with oils,
should cave open for her beloved
beneath spice-breathing cedars of Lebanon –
Oh how heaven ached down on his skull.

II

Not angels, trawling the roof with thick
velvet cloaks, howling with friction,
forced unwilling into time and place.
Just gales, the hot-rubbing hands
of opposing plates of air, big as land
masses, bigger; cuffing the house.

Hosea had asked for serious weather
as a sign – Hurricanes from Borneo
that could swell the windows
like bubbles through hoops with soap water –
what he got was force eight, fresh gale,
and an ill-fitting frame's uneasy wail.

III

In rain, or on days without weather,
Hosea Thomas watched from his living-room
as a glow moved hand to mouth
down the burnt-out buffet-car
washed up onto the sidings like spume,
its passengers waiting to set off south

to the hot lands. 'So why', said Hosea
on such days, 'Why do they have to drag
their lives like dead pals behind them?
And why did Gomer give me up to shag
those others? I know we're all to blame
but can't you rope in the leeway?'

IV

'Take me alone, jet me as I speak
far beyond my own earshot, over the backs
of Skiddaw and Blencathra to a ruined
sheepfold, quiet as a steady bell.
Strip me of people and lead me blind
into desert, silent but for my shoes' pestle.'

Hosea frightened himself – this prayer
if cast in solids would fling
friends, downs, ups all out of reach.
He would have two scenes left: exterior,
grass or sand; interior, his soft, shrinking
head, infested with termite language.

God's children left the buffet-car at eight,
picked across the sidings trailing white
from tobacco and bloody cold. Hosea Thomas
kept a lookout down the girder-strong
diagonal ship-canal at the gasometers –
a clump of rusting iron lungs.

With their imperceptible push they pressed
gas through gaps in radiators, up through grids
on streets, rings on cookers. He gagged, put on
the standard-issue mask he had kept in case.
His chest needled as he felt for symptoms –
'Oh God, how did I get like this?'

In the bare night Hosea counted up his ills
of spirit. He found he had sufficient
to see off a thick-skinned saint –
'Why make us when you knew full well we'd fall?'
Sometimes he felt like a brittle-boned
child left to play on a building site alone.

'As you know at times I ache for the heady
heights of sin, finding them rich red.
Like a bigamist my moves are based on fear
of discovery, emotion, disease, loss, gain,
judgement. If it wasn't for fear I'd sin
till I'd drunk myself sober, washed on a far shore.'

Hosea Thomas wondered where a sign
from God might slot into his daily routine.
He'd hoped a dazzling angel might appear
in the two garden sheds knocked into one
where he bred canaries for heaven –
'Don't look so worried, I've come for your birds.'

His worry was that if the angel did not show
but rather spoke, then he might never know.
(A great bell in the foundry once flew down
and clappered him. Hosea heard it still –
his every thought tuned to its monotone.)
'I don't want to meet you, but I do will it.'

Sometimes Hosea Thomas enjoyed the gap
between himself and God as also
the gap between his house and the railway.
True, both were bleak, patchy like bad shaves –
a few strewn cans and objets de scrap,
but both gaps gave him space to grow,

think things through, find his own way.
This was on the good days though, on bad days
he'd buy cantaloupes, slit them into moons and suck
out their smiles. If that failed, winged panic
sent him scurrying over scrap to the buffet-car,
begging advice from the beggars.

Two whole days of unswerving rain –
'Lord, we are like fish that never thought
of water until yanked asthmatic out.
We have hummed with fingers in our ears,
we have set up sticks and asked them questions,
we have forgotten you, but you wait for us.'

Hosea swallowed hard on nothing, prayed
'Lord, let this be the first spit of a flood,
withdraw and let us gape at the pale
powdered hands of the abyss, unlined palms open.'
One in the buffet-car tugged the communication
cord to try to stop the rain – which failed.

X

No go-between came for his canaries,
so heaven's breeder lit some incense in the shed
to put them on the scent, and propped the door.
Some he never glimpsed again, and trusted
that they'd fit the bill above. Others
built no hide around failure.

He saw them polka-dot the railside scrub
like lemon-peel – brilliant alarms bred
for paradise, plugged in patternless mud.
Whenever his doorbell rang, Hosea prayed
'Let this be Gomer back. I can smell
the must, talc, breath mooching up the hall.'

In the dead hours Hosea left a hole
in his dream floor and bumped awake to find
his room an unfamiliar colour.
They had built a fire outside the buffet-car.
On its tongue-tips a dense, black swirl
from burning tyres drove cars in the mind.

'How could such light produce such darkness?'
He watched until the fire had laid its egg
in his brain. He turned and blinked a pattern
on the walls. God's children stank to heaven,
wet clothes warmed to life, dogs curled in dozes.
'How close I've skirted being them, how close.'

XII

Hosea's crest fell, visibly, as soon as
he opened the front door. Gomer, Gomer,
his wife, warm and puffed from her brisk
walk in the chill was once again not there.
A man was. Raw veins mapped a delta on his face.
He'd made a skin cage of his fingers –

'We think these must be yours,'
and then the cage was hands again – numb
and bulbous from a life of clinging –
the canary *en route* upstairs.
The two men shuffled, as if about to sing.
Hosea said 'Thank you for bringing him home.'

Hosea Thomas vowed to be a fool for God
no more. He was sickened by the slide
show on the back of his mind of Gomer stuffed
with other men, and him, the doting husband
squeezing her hand at the bedside.
'Why linger at dinner when there's nothing left?'

That night he dreamt his kid-lipped wife's
return, dress snagged with spores of outside –
street smoke, take-aways, perfume of chill.
To staunch humming hearts he made a welcome meal.
When Hosea woke he was spinning inside,
his soul was an otter: sleek, rare, lithe.

VANISHING POINT

Today the air is like thick soup,
so as we stroll down a tarmac road
that pulls at our feet, we step
up from the ground and float.

Just as a flight through a room
is like a swim in syrup for a fruit
fly, its body being so light,
so it is for us this afternoon,

between two towering rows
of Lombardy poplars that somewhere,
the horizon perhaps, or the coast,
or the end of the continent, blur

into a single line, a last tree.
The vanishing point remains,
continually unwatchable, the same.
Despite our speed, we never see

the point itself, though our
agility was only known before
in dreams, prefiguring the motion
of bodies in glory, sky like ocean.

TO SKIN A TREE

He caught a rainbow trout,
a six-inch clot of light and water.
The hook became the fastened mouth,
barbed.

He could not free, or kill it,
he could only watch it bristle,
changing colour as it dried to death,
and he, more slowly, dried towards it.

He buried it, with colours fixed fast
pale, beneath the silver birch.

By Autumn, it had rotted up the roots,
and now the trunk was peeling bark
like silver scales.

Last Autumn, bark was paper.
This time, fish.
There is more than one way
to skin a tree.

LOCUST PEOPLE

As the liner drifted out with waving
on the decks and shouts like ticker tape,
he was in his cabin, doing sums.

That swarm a plane saw breeding
in a Kalahari bowl would be multiplying
constantly as he sailed towards it.

The ship was steeped in café society,
a chunk of civilisation cut and floated
out to colonise the oceans

with kid leather and shot silk,
pearls which rolled like marbles off decks
down to rediscover shells.

He tried to surmise at which point
of his journey the swarm would grow so
large that numbers became square miles.

Later, driving for weeks into a blaze
of desert, he would use ingenious means
to keep the truck going despite.

When he reached them, he would camp
on the outskirts and observe
the seepage surround and pass him.

At night he would dwell on breeding,
conjure up a warm body from drops
of saliva in the cooling sand.

To fight the daytime heat he would
think of his home town, tainted by
its Dolly Blue works, still in his veins.

He began to kill them, one by one,
for scientific purposes, then food,
impaled on sticks, cracked over fire.

The swarm turned plague at some stage,
but it grew, like faith, he thought,
too gradually to measure –

discernible only when compared with
the previous day, the previous hour –
outstripping the power of integers.

STOP FORTNIGHT

Orange streetlights give way to real flames,
a glut, screaming from slim organ pipes
to burn up the night sky. Fatter chimneys
hold their bellies in, seduce clouds.
The first kiss lingers in the windless dark.

You have come down from the bleaks
like a moth to find the source of orange,
following the glow of ICI, British Steel.
You drive with an ever stronger sweet sulphurous
smell poking in through your window.

It's easy to get lost in the bloodstream
of this huge estate; road, rail and dock
capillaries blocked by striped barriers,
and security guards who say you're miles out,
send you unwinding the same roundabouts.

Crack the maze and you find you're on
a narrowing road, dodging potholes.
On one side, rough stuff is scorched into steel;
on the other, mud flats and sea, catching pale
shines off the howling steelworks floodlights.

You press on, noting through the fence that
with those floods, the flames, and a cascade
of sparks at the moment of truth,
they've found a way of turning orange here.
You bask, but the fence gives you tiger-stripes.

You get a job inside, chiselling out furnaces
on stop fortnight, but they make you wear
asbestos uniforms, wood shoes, and pull
you out at the end of each ten-minute stint
for a break to bring your temperature back.

But even so you're at the source,
an anti-astronaut, each day staying in
a little longer, loosening your clothes
as you wade through knee-high still-hot filings
in the neon glowing flues.

And each time you climb back inside
you hope to find some proof at last
– a baby sleeping deep in the hot swarf –
and to bring it out from the orange heart
into the big blue open.

MALCHUS

First victim of Christendom's violence
against the will of Christ, meant
to defend him from his world. Malchus,
sufferer of the briefest of losses,
an ear cut off to foil an abduction
– since used as the proof of one –
then an immediate healing, the whole
scene like a plane that flies so low
it blocks the afternoon sun for an instant
then releases it. Uneasily impenitent,
he wears this new ear for the rest
of his life, uncertain whether to trust
the sounds it gives him, half wishing
he was deaf, but half still listening.

SIMONE AND THE
UNKNOWN FRIEND

I VIDEO GAMES WITH SIMONE WEIL

Myopic, straining at the screen through pinched,
round lenses, smooth fingers on the joystick
and fire button, Simone, thin as a marble sculpture
pared too far, rocks on her small scuffed shoes
back and forward with the play.

This is willing slavery. That's why she's here,
in a crappy arcade in Torquay out of season,
slowly getting hooked so she will understand
their absolute pinpoint aim on the present –
past forgotten and no future to look on to,

how to exorcise ill-fortune by affording it
no interest, so in the end it shrugs off home,
and the way the slow guilt gets you
as the change man shunts another shaky column
through an arch in the glass and you don't know

how much you've spent, or have left to spend,
or what the time is or even how it's shaped –
fanning out from now like a spray of ack-ack,
or cruising past like the cars in Formula One,
dodging haybales and photographers.

i

I was in a sense midwife to my sister's work.
Under the dining-table I taught her to read
as a birthday present for father. We shared
a birth in logic. Her mind seemed so pure,
rigorous, but even then she must have had a speck
of laxness in her mathematics, like a mite
of plaster that can burst a great clay vessel
in the kiln. It was that speck she valued.
She let it grow into a white statue.
I am mystified by all her talk of God.

ii

Simone our daughter left us in New York.
She loved us but she felt a duty to the world.
She wanted front-line nurses parachuted in
to break the enemy with bold love, tactics of care.
I knew she was unhappy though she played
with Harlem's children like they were her own.
She looked thin at the harbour. Friends said
her soul was approaching transparency. I call
it wasting away. Like a little boat bobs and tugs
at its mooring she did and did not want to let us go,
and walk aboard the Valaaren. When she said
if she had two lives she would give us a whole one
I knew it was the last thing I would ever hear her say.

She sleeps on deck, suspicious of luxury,
told me the story of Mary who found a cottage
in the forest with two doors; one gold, one tar.
Mary said the tar door was good enough for her,
but was showered with gold when she went in.
Simone is showered only by the rain and sea all night.
Tarpaulin can't protect her from these elements.
I think she likes me because I'm a scout,
and I run games for the refugee children.

I have made three friends on board ship.
A scout, a classics teacher and a mental defective.
They are the only ones who resemble themselves.
I saw a woman at dinner tonight cut open a fish
with her silver knife held in a white kid glove.
I have always held fish as a symbol of the faith
but she showed me, pressing out eggs with the blade
(many within one body) and forking them
into her mouth, that symbols are not to be trusted.
They blush and give themselves to any sweet-talker.

i

Two women eating apple fool on a sickbed.
One finishes the bowl, the other a spoonful,
enough to summon childhood's orchards,
and to reinforce an envy of its name.
Koch's bacilli thrive within one – writing TB
across her lungs – and horrify the other,
keeping her distance; can they fly, ride on
a cough, on a breath through a smile?
The fool's a last attempt to feed the French girl.
'Please Simone, or you'll never beat them.'
'We should learn from idiots, not eat them.
Having their skins off means they cannot lie.'

ii

One April Fool's Day I was driving up
Combe Hill when I noticed a figure swinging
from the gibbet, an exclamation mark
on the landscape. I could hear the creaks
of rope on wood before I reached earshot.
I could see his feet, toecaps tapping,
trace incriminating letters on the grass,
and his downstaring ache to be underground.
It was a good fake, a sack painted and dressed,
perpetrators on buzz-bikes in the valley,
one with a chalk pebble in the tyre tread,
telling tales. Inside the sack was a body.

If the first thing you saw was not the flaky
ceiling of your parents' Boulevard de Strasbourg home,
or the red upside-down face of Mme Zeitlin,
the grim midwife, then it must have been before –
a streak of light that tempted you, pulled
you into the huge, firm hands.

If the last thing you saw was not the ivory
glint from an August afternoon on a drip-marked
sink in the sanatorium – taps poised, pipes like roots
in search of water, then there may never be one.
All we see is a lit taper, as much as we can take,
before light gobsmacks open.

HANG-GLIDERS

One Sunday, nothing moved in the high fields
except a few like us, dressed for gales,
craning at the hang-gliders' tight membranes.

The next, each field was quick with hares,
chocolate hares, hot-earth-coated.
They queued in racks on the truck backs.

By dark, the trucks were full and left,
the hares' heads swinging. Hang-gliders
tagged above like huge equatorial insects.

The air creaked above our car, you said
'They can't land. Can't see where to.
They have to wait until it's light.'

THE TELEX

Some nights we get African heat
here, this being one. Too hot to move,
we listen to the huge propellers
loping round above, their revolutions
so constant we wish electricity
had moods.

The blinds are tilted downwards,
eyelids, letting stripes fall
on the floor, making bands of light
and dust across the room
in which insects may be trapped,
even birds.

The street outside is a mile straight,
lined with dark-fronted houses
like this one. It pretends to carry
on then ends with a fence
and a field. Canal and rail from then
on out.

In these temperatures it's good
to hear your memories of Egypt,
how the afternoons were so hot
you had to lie low with the radio.

How even here a secretary
at your factory in the forest took
lunch in the sun and sent a telex
to God when she got back.

THE ALLOTMENT

In the mornings I wake, walk and dig.
In the afternoons I cut and dry;
evenings I consume.
I am the one with caked root hands
and dry black nails.
This is the muck I was born from, into;
it is here that I prepare the ground
to take me whole, so I can be the soil
that dries on your youthful,
burrowing fingers.

This is the open, naked girl
ripped from a magazine left
on the allotments. My digging
was delayed by rain, I watched her
mouth fill up with water,
and her legs, funnelling.
She held a look of ecstasy
as I spaded her into the mud;
fuel for later.

I like to get here early
before the others come.
The dogs come first and then
the hollow rumbling of empty barrows.
By the time they arrive
my patch is like a jungle,
I have soil as rich as blood.
It is slicking sweetly through my veins.

This is the child who's been
missing since . . .
This is the child who was
beaten lifeless, left in a quiet river,
washed up on to the edge of the soil.
I had seen her running away
with the man whose cold hands
were printed on her neck when I found her.
Within a day she was part of my soil.
Her crop was young, fresh and green.
For a whole day the allotment
burst and was cut.
The girl rose through my tending,
then there was nothing – barren.

I am the man who can tame the earth,
can make it rise through
my little patch of ground.
My spade is charmed.
Every dusk I wheel a mountain home,
of skin and bones.
Flesh for the sleepless.
Smokeless fuel for the quiet man's night.

WASPS CARRY OFF THE MEMORIES OF AN OLD WOMAN

The queen selects a nest in spring,
drones and workers follow, and it builds.
They take the lightest memories first,
so soon she says –
'The longest vistas are the clearest,
I can see horizons, mountains, islands
all around, but cannot see if I am
on a boat, balcony, shoreline, valley.'

Her brother sprays the hole
between the outhouse bricks and tiles,
leaves the wasps' gateway framed
in white foam, so none can pass
without the midas-touch of death,
bringing to the queen a fragrant gift;
or flying out across the backyard
in confusion to drop on flagstones
and corrugated roofs like young rain.

The workers – barren females –
have no time for grandmothers.
Not called like bees to match-make
for creation, wasps are go-betweens
for chaos, trapping her ideas
as they rise, in combs of wood
and paper pulped up with saliva,
releasing each one high and streets away.

She envies them their colony,
their clear parameters – job for a year,
set up early, work for a summer,
slow down in autumn then die,
with a fat queen growing
all of next year inside her,
warm and asleep as the future should be.
She asks her brother to leave them alone –
'I'm not your brother, I'm your son.'

THE HOOKSES

Given name
of the sea's
        cuspid row
rocks that warn
         of what they do
  a trawler's corpse
part-clothed   by low tide
  boat cooked in brine
     till the meat fell off:

Hookses
      sun-deck
for cormorants
        to dry wet wings
scarecrow fish wardens:

Getting even
        with Adam
this name picks
      its own objects
  water pushed
       by vast

Atlantic weight
  splits on the rocks
turns into Hookses bay:

Ashore
      from beach
               to high farm
all was taken by this name
      so long ago
that in rare dealings
   with the wide
          collapsing world
the fifteen souls
           who made
this distant farm
      their island
           within land
give full name and address
as simply
           Hookses.

Made of one long oblong slab
of warm white – sheerest white
with a concentrated drop of red
mixed in – its shadow a misshapen
black tablecloth laid on the grass.

Our terrace is a border, a lookout
post, an open cell, but more
it is the place where we can meet
the whole created order halfway,
and neither side be dominant.

We are a community of outcasts
from a nation of outcasts –
whilst we sit on the terrace,
the sun picks through our house
displacing dust, examining.

Behind blue railings that are always
warm in their seven flaking layers,
we can look across the garden –
stream, pond, lawn, bracken and spikes,
then over cliffs which cave inland.

At spring tide – lowest of the year –
we slide down their scree,
balletically teeter out to new pools
only visible on this day
when waves draw so far back.

Madonna of the Rocks – what richness!
Thick straps of kelp glinting on bare
stone backs – clear or purple jellies
with their tracery of entrails –
made with no one looking.

Fresh limpets bedding down,
and stars and sidling crabs,
their nakedness soon to be covered –
and one impossibly perfect
triangular pool in terracotta rock –

An underwater meadow –
green waves through its fingers
like a field of wheat.
Shells dry and sharpen on the terrace,
and the dog checks them out –

gentle sniffing and taste of salt.
Around them ants create
an urgent imperceptible geometry,
and the stone floor, which could be
anything today, ticks and settles.

At the brink of light and dark
we often all come out on to
a cooler terrace, lanterns round
its fading edges, to talk
of stewardship, of running worlds –

our deeper voices smack against
the wall of the house and seem
to echo round the emptying bay –
seabirds and fish rinsed
out by heavenly darkness.

And even in broad day
there's always at least one
of us braving the white-hot terrace,
glancing out to sea over a book
simply for the sake of ceremony –

Unquestioned, though no longer
needed, because no one lands,
nor would. But watching waves
can show the painstaking slowness
of the course of history –

how continents were conquered
by a row of white sails
that silently grew from the sky,
so a fisherman had time to pull
in nets and join his frightened people.

At that pace our life changed
last winter. Children playing
on the terrace found a big dog
ambling down the garden path,
a sack of paper tied to its collar.

It was supposed to wander
past our smallholding, out
to the plains beyond – to starve,
die, rot, and take into the earth
the sins of those who sent it.

Our children called him 'Goat'
for obvious reasons, and because
we wished he was, so we could
tie it to the terrace rail and drink
its milk, then kill and roast it

for the resurrection supper
on Easter Sunday. We still keep
all the festivals and sabbaths,
and we pray for those still killed
for keeping them.

Lifted
From the bay
By the ever
              inhaling
Land their long
Evening shadows
Too vast
              and faint
Barely print
On grass embers:
Outstretched above
The coast path
In swathes
In silence
The completion
Of the world
Can wait
Until this
              flight
Is done.

From painting
the boat trailer
strong silver,
from unwinding
clothes the gales
wound on a line,
from clearing
summer growth
in a stream's husk
so when it returns
it can pelt
to the sea unencumbered,
from these and a dozen
more scenes
of small accomplishment
towards the one end
they come inside
to eat a bread meal.
The plates they use,
the gateleg table,
the fabric of the house
so lived in and upon
for many years
grow tougher
with each break
like re-set bone,
each friendship has been
broken and healed
each marriage annulled
and renewed countless
times by choice,
for fear that
in spite of living

on this raw
exposed headland
they might still
leave corners
inaccessible
to new Atlantic light.

Sparse precise thunder
from an inland
bombing range
grows insistent
in an afternoon already
high in menace –
dark sky,
sharp light
becoming water.
Children run
for the house,
drop their games
on the disused coastal
fighter base
where they,
with sheep and gorse,
are steps
in reclamation.
One still
has the cuts
from when
this phoney war began
ten days ago,
she took it for
the birth of a storm
and stayed out
to count seconds
wait for lightning
when – like a skein
of black geese
in the distance,
then like the last
piece of shrapnel

from a blown city –
a camouflaged jet
toppled her into
the green and brown
living and dry
community of thorns,
leaving sound for dead.

Pewter like peeled fruit in its soft cloth
left on a sea and sun-gazed table,
facing Ireland while we walk the cliff.

Christ Jesus circled by four apostles –
below which, pilgrims in bowed procession,
above which, heaven's ecstatic spirals –

but on the brink of war and weddings,
we scour our hearts for more than metal,
as streams from high fields plunge like swine.

With or without wings he is coming
at incredible speed from everywhere
to this baking terrace – to here –
as she pours herself an ice-cold drink
outside a house that rocks on cliffs.
She wears shades, flakes in a deckchair.
A red crescent dries above her lip.

O Gabriel make her waking as gentle
as the eye-blue of a distant sail.
Still she'll drop her half-full glass
in shock and joy at what you ask.
With a choked-up 'yes' it all begins –
the afternoon sea will leap and scale
the cliffs to offer its obedience.

The sun will nuzzle like a pet
at her ankles, and in that twilight
shells will sing the vespers of love,
and momentarily across the globe
the day will check in mid-stride
like it's just stepped off a tube,
looking for bearings, the way up and out.